THE
LORD'S
SUPPER

O lead my blindness by the hand,
lead me to thy familiar feast;
not here and now to understand,
but even here and now to taste
how the eternal Word of heaven
on earth in broken bread is given.

W. E. GLADSTONE
1809–98

THE LORD'S SUPPER

ETERNAL WORD IN BROKEN BREAD

ROBERT LETHAM

P U B L I S H I N G

P.O. BOX 817 • PHILLIPSBURG • NEW JERSEY 08865-0817

Page design by Tobias Design
Typesetting by Michelle Feaster

Printed in the United States of America

Library of Congress Cataloging-in-Publication Data

Letham, Robert.
     The Lord's Supper : eternal word in broken bread / Robert Letham.
          p.   cm.
     Includes bibliographical references and index.
     ISBN 0-87552-202-5 (pbk.)
     1. Lord's Supper. 2. Lord's Supper—Presbyterian Church. 3. Lord's Supper—Reformed Church. I. Title.

BV825.2.L49 2001
234'.163'08825—dc21

                                                                2001024727

For *"all those who, in every place,*
call upon the name of the Lord Jesus"
(Westminster Confession of Faith 26.2)
and in particular
for the session and congregation
of Emmanuel Orthodox Presbyterian Church,
Wilmington, Delaware,
who have helped to make the years since 1989
especially enjoyable and fruitful.

CONTENTS

There is nothing in this world, or out of this world, more to be wished by every one of you than to be conjoined with Jesus Christ, and once for all made one with Him, the God of glory. This heavenly and celestial conjunction is procured and brought about by two special means. It is brought about by means of the Word and preaching of the Gospel, and it is brought about by means of the Sacraments and their ministration. The Word leads us to Christ by the ear; the Sacraments lead us to Christ by the eye. . . . But there is one thing that you must always remember: there is no doctrine either of the simple Word or of the Sacraments, that is able to move us if Christ takes away His Holy Spirit. Therefore whenever you come to hear the doctrine, whether it be of the Sacraments or of the simple Word, ask that God may be present by His Holy Spirit.

ROBERT BRUCE
The Mystery of the Lord's Supper
1590

INTRODUCTION

Nothing presents a starker contrast between our own day and the Reformation than the current neglect of the Lord's Supper. In the century of the Reformation the Supper was the single most commonly discussed topic. Protestants and Roman Catholics alike spilled more ink over this than over justification by faith or the authority of the Bible. It was the litmus test that defined a man's religion. Martyrs such as Cranmer, Latimer, Ridley, and Hooper were burned at the stake for their denial of the Roman dogma of transubstantiation. In turn, intramural Protestant polemics focused on the Lord's Supper more than on any other single issue. Volume upon volume debated, defined, and attempted to explain the manner of Christ's presence in the sacrament.

Yet today, the communion hardly features as a matter of significance. It is seen as an optional extra. Often it is treated casually, as a pleasant and cozy ceremony. Some argue against churches holding it frequently on the basis that familiarity breeds contempt. In part at least, this is due to the long-term effect of

1

INTRODUCTION

the eighteenth-century revivals and the birth of evangelicalism. These were a reaction against a decaying church. In turn, a Christian became defined as someone who could lay claim to a definite personal experience of conversion. The immediate work of the Holy Spirit on the individual soul was thrust onto center stage. The church and sacraments were relegated to secondary importance. Often they were seen to divide people who shared the same direct experience of the regenerating power of the Holy Spirit. All this took place while a seismic shift occurred in Western culture toward the individual. Corporate activities and structures came to be seen as having a dampening influence on vital individual, personal experience.

In time, Presbyterian and Reformed churches were infiltrated by such thinking. When, in the 1840s, John Nevin of Mercersburg expounded the classic Reformed teaching on the Lord's Supper, he was trenchantly opposed by some of the appointed guardians of that very theology, such as Charles Hodge. The verdict of history has been that Nevin was right and that Hodge had failed to grasp his own theological tradition. Hodge never attempted a reply to Nevin's classic hundred-page article on the Reformed doctrine of the Lord's Supper, an article that established itself as standard for a hundred years.[1]

Today, those in this tradition have neglected this centrally important matter, something bequeathed to the church by Jesus Christ. The teaching of The Westminster Confession of Faith in chapter 29 rarely features large in even the most vigilant of Presbyterians' examination of ministerial candidates. Publishers' catalogs have very few works on the Lord's Supper, and those listed were usually written in previous centuries. The pages that follow will seek to demonstrate how tragic is this neglect and how imperative it is that it be remedied.

ONE

BIBLICAL FOUNDATIONS OF THE LORD'S SUPPER

Jesus instituted the Lord's Supper on the night he was betrayed. Details are recorded in the Synoptic Gospels, in Matthew 26:20–30, Mark 14:17–26, and Luke 22:14–23. Paul records the word of institution in 1 Corinthians 11:23ff. as follows:

> For I received from the Lord what I also passed on to you: the Lord Jesus, on the night he was betrayed, took bread, and when he had given thanks, he broke it and said, "This is my body, which is for you; do this in remembrance of me." In the same way, after supper he took the cup, saying, "This cup is the new covenant in my blood; do this, whenever you drink it, in remembrance of me." For whenever you eat this bread and drink this cup, you proclaim the Lord's death until he comes.

These are well-known words, but they lead to a raft of questions.

The Lord's Supper and Passover

Often the Last Supper is thought to be the Passover meal. As a result, a direct connection is perceived to exist between the Passover and the Lord's Supper. The Passover was held annually from 6 P.M. 14 Nissan to 6 P.M. 15 Nissan to commemorate Israel's deliverance from Egypt on the night the destroying angel passed over the firstborn in Israel and acted in judgment on those in Egypt. It was an occasion when the children were taught about this great deliverance.

However, was this so? Was the Lord's Supper so directly in line with the Passover feast of old Israel? For a number of reasons this is not so evident as is sometimes supposed. First, we are less sure now than we once were about the precise origins of many worship practices in the early church. As Paul Bradshaw has indicated, the connection is at best tenuous. Moreover, even if it *were* a Passover meal, none of the eucharistic practices of the early church can clearly be traced back to the Passover.[1] At most the connection would be academic.

Second, the Last Supper did not occur on the night the Passover was celebrated. John 18:28 indicates that the Passover was, in fact, on the following day and that while Jesus was on trial (later than the supper he and the disciples had eaten) the Jews were still in the throes of preparation for the next day's Passover meal. Certainly, Paul describes Jesus as "our Passover" offered for us (1 Cor. 5:7), but he refers to Jesus' death the next day, not to the meal the previous night. In this sense, there was a clear connection between these events and the Passover but the point of contact was not the Supper but the cross.[2]

Third, the clearest connection with the Old Testament is not with the Passover but with the covenant meal eaten by Moses and Aaron, Nadab and Abihu, and the seventy elders of Israel on the top of Mount Sinai (Exod. 24:1–11). Moses took half of the blood of the burnt offerings and fellowship offerings and sprinkled it on the altar; the rest he put in bowls. He read the Book of the Covenant, and then sprinkled the remaining blood on the people, saying, "This is the blood of the covenant." Then the leaders of Israel climbed the mountain, saw the God of Israel, and ate and drank. This was a fellowship meal with the God of Israel. Jesus' words of institution clearly reflect this scene, when he says, "This is my blood of the new covenant."[3]

New Testament Terminology

There are a number of terms used in the New Testament to describe the sacrament. Each expresses a different dimension of its meaning. At the same time, no one of them sums up the totality of biblical teaching on the Supper.

(1) In Acts (2:42; 20:7)[4] it is called *the breaking of bread*. Here is an obvious reference to the action of taking the bread and breaking it. Since Jesus had described the bread as his body, the implication is that this is a graphic portrayal of his death on the cross, where his body was broken to secure our redemption.

(2) In 1 Corinthians 10:21 Paul speaks of *the Lord's table*, and of the incompatibility of participating in sacrifices offered to demons and at the same time in the table of the Lord. In view here is the reality that this is a rite that belongs to Christ. He instituted it. He presides at it. The table at which it occurs is his. Therefore those who sit with him at this table cannot also take part in tables devoted to false deities.

(3) In 1 Corinthians 11:20 Paul calls the meal *the Lord's Supper*. Once again he reminds us of the one who owns and presides over the covenant meal.

(4) In 1 Corinthians 10:16–17 Paul refers to the cup and the

bread of this supper as a *participation* or *communion* in the body and blood of Christ. The word he uses—*koinōnia*—can mean fellowship, participation in, or communion. It denotes a common purpose or identity. However, it means more than simply a common association such as in a typical human activity like a sports team.

(5) A fifth term occurs in the record of the institution of the Supper (Matt. 26:26–27; Mark 14:22–23; Luke 22:17–19; 1 Cor. 11:23–24). Jesus "took bread, gave thanks [*eucharisteō*], broke it and said . . ." The Greek verb *eucharisteō* means to give thanks, and it is from this that the English liturgical term *eucharist* derives. The Lord's Supper is a thanksgiving. Jesus gave thanks to the Father for the impending offering of his own flesh on the cross. In turn, we give thanks to the Father in and through his Son by the Holy Spirit for all that he did for us there and continues to do now that he has risen from the dead.

What Happens in the Eucharist

There are three main things that happen when the Lord's Supper takes place.

(1) *It is a memorial.* Jesus says, "Do this in remembrance of me." This is the most commonly noted of all, largely because it is the easiest to understand. It refers to something self-evidently in our own power. We all know how to remember past events. In this case, the focus of our minds is on Jesus Christ, his self-sacrificial love, his death on the cross for our sins, his resurrection, and his continuing intercession on our behalf. Many limit the Lord's Supper to this one aspect. The vast bulk of evangelicals and even many Reformed view it exclusively as a memorial. However, much more than this is involved.

(2) The Lord's Supper is itself *a proclamation of the gospel.*

Paul stressed that whenever the Supper is held we "proclaim the Lord's death until he comes" (1 Cor. 11:26). Augustine described this vividly when he wrote of the sacraments as "a kind of visible word" of God.[5] Whereas the preaching of the Word brings the gospel of God's grace to our ears, the sacraments portray it before our eyes. In the Lord's Supper we see before us a loaf of bread torn to pieces. Even so Christ's body was, so to speak, torn to shreds for our salvation, to make us whole. Again, as the wine is poured into a cup so Christ's blood was poured out unto death that we might receive life. In this way God appeals to other senses than through preaching. These are, indeed, his appointed visual aids to reinforce the word we hear. Even this, however, does not exhaust the meaning of the sacrament.

(3) Paul calls the eucharist *"communion"* or *"participation" in the body and blood of the Lord* (1 Cor. 10:16–17). For a more detailed understanding of what this means we must take a closer look at Jesus' own teaching in John 6. For now we can summarize by saying that it relates to our union with Christ and its cultivation by the Holy Spirit as we eat and drink the physical elements.

Jesus as the Bread of Life (John 6:47–58)

> "I tell you the truth, he who believes has everlasting life. I am the bread of life. Your forefathers ate the manna in the desert, yet they died. But here is the bread that comes down from heaven, which a man may eat and not die. I am the living bread that came down from heaven. If anyone eats of this bread he will live for ever. This bread is my flesh, which I will give for the life of the world."

> Then the Jews began to argue sharply among them-
> selves, "How can this man give us his flesh to eat?"
> Jesus said to them, "I tell you the truth, unless you
> eat the flesh of the Son of Man and drink his blood, you
> have no life in you. Whoever eats my flesh and drinks
> my blood has eternal life, and I will raise him up at the
> last day. For my flesh is real food and my blood is real
> drink. Whoever eats my flesh and drinks my blood re-
> mains in me, and I in him. Just as the living Father sent
> me and I live because of the Father, so the one who
> feeds on me will live because of me. This is the bread
> that came down from heaven. Your forefathers ate
> manna and died, but he who feeds on this bread will live
> for ever."

Some argue that this passage is not sacramental. Two main factors appear to support this position. (1) Jesus spoke these words
before he gave instructions about the eucharist. His speech here
would have made no sense if he intended it to refer to the Supper. (2) To interpret it as sacramental leads us to view his statement about eating his flesh and drinking his blood as
tantamount to cannibalism, which is not only unacceptable but
is, frankly, ridiculous. I will leave discussion of the second of
these two arguments until our detailed exegesis of the passage.
For now let us consider the first, the claim that it would have
been anachronistic of Jesus to have referred to a sacrament he
had not yet introduced.

First, while the institution of the Lord's Supper did not occur until after the events described here, nevertheless from
John's perspective (as the compiler of the Fourth Gospel), looking back on the life, ministry, death, and resurrection of Jesus as
a whole, he saw Jesus' speech as directly connected to the later

introduction of the sacrament. From his later authorial stand-point the two were in effect part of the same reality.

Second, there are other instances in the Gospels where Jesus mentions events before they actually occur. Frequently he refers to his coming death and resurrection, although his disciples had not the faintest idea what he was talking about. Moreover, he discusses the persecution the church was to face, the impending destruction of Jerusalem, the discipline the church was to exercise over its members, and the very existence of the church itself long before those things came to be.[6] In view of this, there is no reason why he could not have done the same in connection with the Supper.

Third, the preceding narrative of the feeding of the five thousand is couched in similar language to the Synoptic Gospels' description of the institution of the eucharist. At the Last Supper Jesus took bread, gave thanks, bróke it, and distributed it (Luke 22:19; Matt. 26:26–27; Mark 14:22–23). Here, with the assembled crowds sitting on the ground, he takes the loaves, gives thanks, and distributes them (John 6:11). The parallel is close but not exact. There is sufficient correspondence, however, to suggest a possible allusion to the Lord's Supper. We recall also that a common theme in early Christian art was the association of the eucharist with the theme of multiplication and that frequently this theme was directly associated with this feeding miracle.[7]

Fourth, the following section portrays apostasy by many erstwhile disciples in the light of the "hard saying" of the bread of life discourse (vv. 60–71). At the conclusion Jesus refers to Judas as the only one of the Twelve who will defect. This recalls the events at the Last Supper itself, when Judas, having received the bread, stalked out of the room to betray Jesus.

Fifth, as we shall see in what follows, the only way to make sense of the hard saying on eating Jesus' flesh and drinking his blood is to see it in the light of the eucharist. Indeed, the early church was accused, among other things, of cannibalism and incest since they often spoke of eating Christ's flesh and drinking his blood in the context of love-feasts at which they were all brothers and sisters.[8] In the first few centuries of the church this passage was generally understood to refer to the eucharist.

In fact, many scholars who doubt a sacramental reference to the passage nevertheless end up recognizing that what Jesus teaches here finds its fullest expression precisely in the eucharist. Among these are the Baptists George Beasley-Murray and D. A. Carson.[9]

The Context

Having fed the five thousand, Jesus reflects on the miraculous feeding of the Israelites by Yahweh in the desert. He then asserts that he fulfills this event. Jesus is the bread of life, given by the Father to sustain his people through their earthly pilgrimage (John 6:25–40). He is the one who has come to feed and nourish us. God's nourishment for us is found in Jesus. Furthermore, this nourishment is eternal (vv. 37–40). All that the Father has given to him will come to him. This coming to him is equivalent to believing in him (v. 37). Those who believe will not be cast out—an idiom called *litotes*, which affirms a matter by denying its opposite, meaning here that the Father will receive them and preserve them. As a result, those who have eternal life will all persevere in faith. None will be lost. At the last day they will all be raised from the dead.

Jesus Is Received Through Faith (John 6:41–47)

In response to these claims, the Jews grumble, not unlike Israel in the desert, before them. How could this man make claims like this when he came from a place like Nazareth? In response to this stark unbelief and consternation, Jesus points out that faith is a gift of God (vv. 44–47). The Father draws us to faith. By nature, we are unwilling to believe. Even if miracles were performed before our eyes, like the feeding of the five thousand, we would be unable to believe because of our sinful nature. Only the Father is able to break down this hostility. Jesus the bread of life is received through faith, and this is the result of the Father's gracious gift.

Jesus Is Eaten and Drunk in the Lord's Supper (John 6:48–58)

Jesus goes on to say that the bread is his flesh given for the life of the world. He is evidently referring to his death on the cross. This was the great goal of his life and ministry. The Word became flesh in the incarnation (1:14). The purpose of the incarnation was the atonement, in which he lay down his life for the world. In his flesh he offered himself up to the Father as a sacrifice for our sins. The bread Jesus gives for our nourishment is himself offered upon the cross. This death was a full human fleshly reality that cannot be toned down. A figurative understanding of the cross is heretical since it destroys the entirety of the Christian faith. Newbigin puts his finger on the pulse of the passage when he remarks that "the deliberately crude and shocking word forces the reader to look beyond the language of the Torah, of teaching and instruction, and to ask 'What more is implied?' " He points to Greek having two words for "body" and "flesh" compared to one in Aramaic. The deliberate use of *sarx* here instead of *sōma* as in the Synoptics "shifts the content of what it means to receive Jesus away from a purely mental and spiritual hearing and believing, in the direction of a physical chewing and swallowing."[10] In short, these are the Johannine equivalents of the words spoken by Jesus at the Last Supper recorded in the other Gospels.

This was scandalous to those who heard it! "How can this man give us his flesh to eat?"(John 6:52). The contempt of the Jewish audience is clear. Their shock and revulsion came since they understood him to refer to cannibalism. If Jesus himself is the bread of life and life comes by eating his flesh, this entails cannibalism. To drink blood was forbidden by the law and, before that, by the legislation given after the flood (Gen. 9:4). Animal blood was to be drained before the meat could be eaten (Lev. 3:17; Deut. 12:23). Still less was human blood acceptable.

However, Jesus makes no attempt to tone his language down or to explain it as merely figurative. On the contrary, he intensifies it. Instead of backing off and pointing out that his hearers had misinterpreted him, he boldly underlines what he had said. They had understood him only too well and their reaction was rational. The eating and drinking, Jesus insists, is very physical indeed! From John 6:54 there is a remarkable change of verb. Hitherto John has used *phagō*, which means simply to eat. Now, however, he switches to *trōgō*, a crude and vulgar word meaning to chew, gnaw, or bite audibly.[11] He uses this verb exclusively throughout the rest of the passage. By choosing it, he draws attention to the physical process of chewing and swallowing and to the audible accompaniments that go with it. This is so in verses 54, 56, and 57, where the verb is used. He underlines further what he has said. Far from appeasing his opponents, he challenges them head on. So much is clear by their ultimate reaction. These words are recognized as "a hard saying" and an unbearable one (vv. 60–66). Many turn away and abandon discipleship. Even the Twelve seem to waver.

What does it mean? It is obvious that Jesus is not advocating real-life cannibalism. But neither can his language be emptied of its raw force. If he had wanted to offset the Jewish hostility, he had every opportunity to do so. But neither he nor they were governed by the philosophy of Plato, which would have enabled them to see these claims in a purely spiritualized dimension. If we view the narrative as connected theologically with the eucharist (and frankly I know of no other way that adequately explains both Jesus' meaning and the audience's response), we can immediately find a solution.

By talking of our eating his flesh and drinking his blood in the Lord's Supper, Jesus shows exactly *how* he is the bread of life, feeding and nourishing us to everlasting life. Christ is to us the bread of life as we feed on him in the eucharist, as we eat his flesh and drink his blood. This means two things so inseparable that they are like two sides of the same coin. Believing on the one hand, eating and drinking on the other—*both* go together and *both* are necessary and indispensable.

First, *we feed on Christ the bread of life through faith.* The eucharist is not some magical rite that automatically conveys the grace of God. As the wilderness generation fell short, and Jesus' opponents also did not believe, so without faith we cannot eat the true bread and so receive eternal life. We cannot eat the Lord's Supper aright apart from faith.

Second, *Christ is the bread of life in the Lord's Supper.* Jesus does not teach magic but neither does he purvey some idealized, spiritual salvation divorced from the flesh. Eating and drinking go together with faith. They are two sides of the same coin. The eucharist is central to the gospel. While the eucharist without faith profits us nothing, so faith without the eucharist is barren and empty. In the Lord's Supper through faith (the gift of the Holy Spirit) we eat Christ's flesh and drink his blood and so are nourished to everlasting salvation.

What are the consequences of eating Christ's flesh and drinking his blood in the Lord's Supper through faith? First, *we are granted union and communion with Christ by the Holy Spirit*

(v. 56). As we eat, food becomes one with us. It enters our system, we digest it, and so we produce energy that enables us to live an active life. So when we eat and drink Christ, he enters our system. He indwells us and, in turn, we remain in him. We grow into union. There is mutual indwelling—he in us his church, we in him. This is a great mystery. We cannot explain any further. Some people scoff at anything not reducible to human logic. What do they know of this? This is a matter more to be adored than investigated. Meanwhile, we can be sure that Christ supplies us with the energy to live for him in this world.

Second, *we are introduced into the living fellowship of the Triune God* (v. 57). The living Father sent the Son. The Father has life in himself. He sent the Son in the incarnation, when the Word became flesh and lived among us (1:14). In turn, he gave the Son to have life in himself (cf. 5:26), so that the Son lives because of the Father. Thus, the Son receives life from the Father. There is an inviolable order within the united and undivided Trinity. Furthermore, we receive life from the Son as we chew him in the eucharist. Has this ever been better expressed than by Calvin?

> Accordingly, he shows that in his humanity there also dwells fullness of life, so that whoever has partaken of his flesh and blood may at the same time enjoy participation in life.
>
> We can explain the nature of this by a familiar example. Water is sometimes drunk from a spring, sometimes drawn, sometimes led by channels to water the fields, yet it does not flow forth from itself for so many uses, but from the very source, which by unceasing flow supplies and serves it. In like manner, the flesh of Christ

is like a rich and inexhaustible fountain that pours into us the life springing forth from the Godhead into itself. Now who does not see that communion of Christ's flesh and blood is necessary for all who aspire to heavenly life?[12]

Third, *we receive eternal life* (John 6:48–51a, 51b, 53–54, 58). Christ gave his flesh for the life of the world. He has eternal life since he *is* eternal life. At the last day we shall be raised from the dead since we are united with him who is the life. This life is poured into us by the Holy Spirit as, in faith, we feed on Christ in the Lord's Supper. It is a pledge to the faithful that we will share in the resurrection at the last day.

Other References or Allusions to the Lord's Supper

In *Luke 24* the two disciples traveling to Emmaus invite Jesus to stay with them since it is getting dark. They are unaware of who he is, supposing Jesus to be dead but yet confused by reports that his grave is empty. Despite the lengthy explanations this stranger gives about the fulfillment of biblical prophecy in the Christ, they are so sad and shocked that they simply do not realize who he is. This continues until, on reaching their home, they prevail upon him to stay overnight. Then,

> when he was at the table with them, he took bread, gave thanks, broke it and began to give it to them. Then their eyes were opened and they recognized him, and he disappeared from their sight. (vv. 30–31)

Note that Luke uses the same formula as he does for the Lord's Supper in 22:19—"he took bread, gave thanks, broke it and [gave] it to them." Of course, this was not an official church celebration of the Supper. Yet it was the Lord's Supper because *the Lord* was there presiding. Moreover, Luke sees it as sharing in the same features. Note the immediate reaction of the two: "Then their eyes were opened, and they recognized him" (v. 31). Jesus is immediately recognized in his Supper. The word, of course, went before, the exposition of the Scriptures (what an exposition that must have been) by the one about whom they testified (v. 32). They race back to Jerusalem to report "how Jesus was recognized by them in the breaking of bread" (v. 35). It is his Supper, he presides, he makes himself known.

In *Revelation* 3:14–20 the risen Christ writes a letter to the church at Laodicea. The church is lukewarm in its allegiance, and Christ warns that unless it repents, he will spew it out of his mouth. At the end (in v. 20) he gives a promise to anyone who will respond to his warning.

> Here I am! I stand at the door and knock. If anyone hears my voice and opens the door, I will come in and have supper with him and he with me.

These words, often taken out of context and made the basis of an evangelistic appeal, are addressed to a church, and so we should visualize a churchly scene. Christ has been shut out of the church by neglect and self-satisfaction on the part of the members. He asks for readmittance, having warned earlier of the dire consequences of the status quo. An allusion to the eucharist is more than likely. If so, Christ speaks of it in terms of fellowship, very close to the idea of communion about which Paul wrote.

In *Revelation* 19:1–8 the consummation of the church's salvation is seen in the wedding supper of the Lamb. The church is the bride, made ready for the Lamb. Christ and the church are united in the context of a great eschatological feast. The similarity of terms between the supper of the Lamb and the supper of the Lord is hardly accidental, for the Lamb is the Lord, as is shown earlier in the book, where the Lion of the tribe of Judah who directs human history is also a Lamb that had been slain (5:1–14). In view of this the whole book points to a connection between the struggling, persecuted churches of Asia Minor and the church triumphant in heaven. The Lord's Supper, in their beleaguered vulnerability, is on a continuum with the supper of the Lamb that the entire church celebrates with Christ in heaven. This echoes the teaching of the Letter to the Hebrews, where the church today is described in its worship as having come "to Mount Zion, to the city of the living God, the heavenly Jerusalem, . . . to Jesus, the mediator of a new covenant and to the blood of sprinkling that speaks better things than the blood of Abel" (Heb. 12:22–24). In the Lord's Supper we join with the church triumphant, "with angels and archangels, and all the company of heaven," in worshiping the risen Christ. Even more, only the church (not the angels or any other creature) has this communion with him.

> We taste thee, O thou living bread,
> and long to feast upon thee still;
> we drink of thee, the fountain head,
> and thirst our souls from thee to fill.
>
> Our restless spirits yearn for thee
> where'er our changeful lot is cast;
> glad when thy gracious smile we see,
> blest when our faith can hold thee fast.

THE LORD'S SUPPER

O Jesus, ever with us stay,
make all our moments calm and bright;
chase the dark night of sin away,
shed o'er the world thy holy light.

Bernard of Clairvaux (1091–1153)

THE LORD'S SUPPER IN CHURCH HISTORY

Physical Presence: Transubstantiation

Following our survey of the New Testament, we should not be surprised that there soon developed a view of the Lord's Supper that saw the body and blood of Christ as present in a physical manner. As early as the second century we find Justin Martyr (d. 155) talking in terms of a realistic corporal presence of Christ in the eucharist.[1] This view developed over the centuries in the Western church and eventually became dogma at the Fourth Lateran Council in 1215.[2] In the East, transubstantiation also held sway. However, due to the emergence and rapid spread of Islam, the Eastern church did not see the developments that occurred in the West but instead was frozen in something of a time warp from the sixth century. Hence, Eastern orthodoxy has made no attempt to *explain* what happens in the eucharist when the elements are changed, preferring to highlight the aspect of mystery.

In the Western or Roman Catholic view, Aristotelian philosophy was used to explain what appears at first glance to be impossible. How can the bread and wine be changed into the actual physical body and blood of Christ when it is obvious to our eyes that they are still the same as they ever were? The Aristotelian distinction between *substance* and *accidents* was the means to resolve this conundrum. The substance of a thing is what that individual thing really is, its intrinsic nature. On the other hand, accidents refer to incidentals, features relating not to a thing's inner nature but more to what it may appear to be, or to something adventitious that could be withdrawn without altering that thing's substance.[3] The works of Aristotle were rediscovered from around 1050 and so proved a fruitful resource for the church. Hence, the bread and wine were held to change into the body and blood of Christ according to substance (hence *trans* = change, *substantia* = of substance), according to what they really were intrinsically, while they remained bread and wine *per accidens*, in terms of accidents or appearances. Certainly they seemed to remain what they had been, while having undergone this change of inner essence. At root, this was not magic but a sacramental mystery. It occurred when the priest consecrated the elements.

It is not hard to appreciate this development if Jesus' teaching in John 6 was sacramental in the sense we described. The most obvious potential misunderstanding would be to view his words in a crassly physical sense. This misunderstanding was effectively a simplification, one that took root at the popular level among the unsophisticated laity. It was fostered by a growing idea that the ministers of the church were priests. In turn, priests offer sacrifices. The priests of the church thus present the eucharist as a sacrifice, one consisting of the body and blood of Christ. These developments went together. As early as the third century we find Origen (185–254) and Cyprian (200–258) both talking of the Lord's Supper as a "eucharistic sacrifice."[4]

Again, the position of the Roman church on the relationship between nature and grace also helped in the development of transubstantiation. According to Rome, grace perfects nature. Natural gifts and gifts from the Holy Spirit are effectively one and the same. In this sense the physical and the spiritual are so closely identified that in practice they are merged into one. From this perspective, it is easy to see how the bread and wine can be said to be the body and blood of Christ and how spiritual grace can be conveyed more or less automatically by physical means.

The early appearance and inexorable development of this teaching is, I suggest, evidence itself to support our interpretation of John 6. It is exceedingly hard to see how this view could put in such an early appearance if the New Testament intended us to think of the eucharist in purely symbolic or figurative terms. On the other hand, its emergence is more readily explained as a distortion of the view we outlined earlier.[5]

Transubstantiation was the doctrine the Reformers opposed. Abandonment of the Mass was the single most decisive event marking the Reformation in its various centers. Many gave their lives rather than submit to its imposition as church dogma. We shall consider whether the martyrs were right to do so shortly, but first we must ask why this teaching is wrong.

First, transubstantiation confuses the sign (bread and wine) with the reality (Christ's body and blood). In the sacraments, there are always these two distinct poles to consider. Christ is presented in the sacraments in the form of physical elements. These latter are signs. Like signposts, which direct us to a destination other than themselves, the sacramental signs point elsewhere. They direct us away from themselves to Christ. At the same time, there is a connection between sign and reality. The elements in the sacraments are appropriate to the reality they represent. In baptism, water visibly represents cleansing from sin. As water cleans our bodies, so in baptism we are cleansed from sin by the grace of Christ. Again, as bread and wine sustain and nourish us physically, so in the eucharist we are nourished by Christ—we feed on him by faith to eternal life. In the case of the Roman Catholic teaching, this connection is stressed at the expense of the distinction. By identifying the signs with the reality Rome has compressed the spiritual and the physical, nature and grace. Put crudely, in the words of C. H. Spurgeon, the result is that divine honors are given to a piece of bread.[6]

Second, a number of inevitable consequences flow from considering a change of substance to occur in the Lord's Supper. For instance, if the bread is now the actual physical body of Christ, it follows that the faithful must worship it. In turn, it is elevated for all to see in order that adoration take place. Again, it follows that any of the sacramental elements left over afterwards must not be thrown away. One cannot drop the body of Christ into a garbage can or allow the blood of Christ to spill on the floor. Hence, the bread is reserved and must be preserved or consumed at a later date in another sacramental observation, while the wine is drunk immediately.

Third, and crucially, the doctrine of transubstantiation short-circuits the need for faith on the part of those who receive the sacrament. If the body and blood of Christ are consumed physically, then all who ingest them receive the grace conveyed *ex opere operato* (by the very fact of the action being performed). By objectifying the sacrament in this physical sense, the onus on the receivers to examine themselves and come to the table with a penitent and believing heart is inevitably offset.[7] Yet Jesus, in John 6, connects the eating and the drinking with believing. We cannot have the one without the other. Moreover, Paul in 1 Corinthians 11 stresses that self-examination is essential in the Supper. That Rome teaches the need for self-examination is, to my mind, despite its doctrine not because of it.[8]

Were, then, the English Reformers misguided to suffer death at the stake rather than subscribe to this teaching? When, the flames glowing white and the heat already singeing his flesh, Hugh Latimer called out his famous words to his fellow bishop Nicholas Ridley, "Be of good comfort, master Ridley, and play the man! We shall this day light such a candle, by God's grace, in England as I trust shall never be put out," had Latimer, with his colleagues (later to be joined by the great Thomas Cranmer), got things out of perspective? Should they not have sought some acceptable compromise? For two reasons I suggest they had little alternative to what they did. In the first place, the political situation of the day forced this dire fate on them. Executions were common in sixteenth-century England, to say the least. It was the most usual way for leading national figures to die. Moreover, at stake was the doctrine of the Church of England and, with it, the future of generations of the faithful. Second, the Marian martyrs recognized correctly that the Lord's Supper was a microcosm of the gospel. One's position on the Supper is an accurate index of one's understanding of the Christian faith as a whole. They saw that the sacrificial context of the Roman dogma of transubstantiation obscured the supreme reality of the once-for-all, finished sacrifice of Christ on the cross. These were questions on which room for acceptable compromise was strictly limited.

Physical Presence: Consubstantiation

For Luther and the Lutheran church, the Lord's Supper is also seen as involving the physical presence of the body and blood of Christ. However, Luther was vehement in rejecting transubstantiation. For him and his followers, the bread and wine remain bread and wine. They undergo no change of substance. However, Luther considered Jesus' words, "This is my body," in a literal sense. At the Colloquy of Marburg (1529), when he, Zwingli, Bucer, and others met to try to reach agreement among themselves in their conflict with Rome, he was insistent on this point, repeatedly scrawling on the table in front of him *"hoc est corpus meum,"* underlining the word *est* (is).[9] Since the bread itself could not be the body, he concluded that Christ was physically present "in, with, and under" the elements. The obvious question here is how this could possibly be.

The solution for the Lutheran view was sought in an innovation concerning the person of Christ. Here Luther argued that there was a transference of divine attributes to the human nature of the incarnate Christ. Thus, among others, the attribute of omnipresence—something that belonged strictly speaking to God alone—was communicated by Christ's divine nature to his human nature in the incarnation. Hence, the risen Christ could be present everywhere not only according to his divine nature but according to his human nature as well. Therefore, he could be present in his body and blood simultaneously wherever the sacrament was celebrated, whether in Wittenberg, Geneva, Strassburg, or wherever.[10]

This ingenious explanation has the feel of being too clever by half. Indeed, it was a definite innovation, for it had no clear precedent in Christian thought. Its ingeniousness was also its Achilles' heel. The point of importance is that, if divine attributes such as omnipresence were communicated to Christ's human nature, how could that human nature still be human? Is not an indispensable aspect of humanity the property of being in only one place at one time? How could a body be omnipresent and still human? In the Lutheran position there are clear hints of the early Christian heresy of docetism, the idea that Christ's humanity was only apparent and not real. In seeking to maintain a physical presence of Christ in the Lord's Supper while rejecting transubstantiation, Luther may have bitten off more than he could chew!

Real Absence: Memorialism

At the other end of the spectrum is the idea that the Lord's Supper is purely symbolic, and that it is solely a memorial of Christ's death. This is the position generally ascribed to the Reformer, Huldrych Zwingli, although there is some doubt as to whether he may have been moving away from it at the time of his premature death. However, it has gained in popularity over the years and is now the most widespread view in evangelical and fundamentalist circles. Many conservative Presbyterians have tended, almost by default, to adopt this position. It is, perhaps, also reinforced by an anxiety among evangelicals not to be identified with Rome. It is an understandable tendency in matters of controversy to seek to distance oneself as far as possible from a position one regards as unacceptable. By viewing the Lord's Supper as simply a symbol, consisting of the purely human action of remembering, one can thereby avoid all possible contamination from association with the dreaded Roman Catholic teaching.

In effect, exponents of this idea deny that there is anything more in the Lord's Supper than the action on the part of the recipients in focusing their minds on Christ and remembering what took place on the cross. The Lord's Supper is not a sacrament in the sense that it is not a channel of grace any more than what occurs in circumstances like prayer or Bible reading. In no sense can Christ be said to be present physically or according to his human nature, since as his body is in one place at one time, he must now be in heaven at the right hand of the Father. To an extent there are clear biblical foundations for what this position affirms. The words of Jesus when he initiated the Supper, "Do this in remembrance of me," unmistakably teach that the eucharist is a memorial.

However, objections to this position relate not to what it affirms but to what it denies. It seems bizarre, to say the least, that if the person of Christ is present everywhere, since he is the Son of God, the stress in the Lord's Supper is on his absence! Moreover, it has difficulty with John 6. It follows that exponents of this view regard this chapter as nonsacramental. Instead, Jesus is referring to us feeding on him by faith. The problem for this viewpoint surrounds Jesus' very realistic and physical statements in that chapter. Given the opportunity to reassure his Jewish hearers that they had misunderstood his teaching and to make it clear that he was talking symbolically, Jesus only reinforces the realistic language even further. His hearers considered him to be speaking in the language of cannibalism, and as a result they left him in disgust. Jesus made no attempt to correct their false impressions. This is the crucial exegetical question to which advocates of a purely symbolic interpretation can scarcely do justice.

There is also a broader philosophical and theological problem here. Zwingli was strongly influenced by neo-Platonism, which held to a dichotomy between the physical and the spiritual realms. Matter was somehow on a lower plane than the world of the spirit. This philosophy had an impact on the church over the centuries and encouraged, among other things, the rise of monasticism. For Zwingli, it meant that he had difficulty in seeing how God's spiritual grace could be channeled through physical means. How could baptism and the Lord's Supper therefore be means of grace? How could Christ be present in a sacrament in which bread and wine were used?[11]

This problem has continued to dog memorialism. It seems to me to rest on a radical separation between the sign and the reality. If Rome confuses the two, the doctrine of the real absence separates them. If Rome virtually identifies natural and spiritual gifts, this position sets them far apart. In so doing, it fails to consider a number of crucial theological matters that intersect with the eucharist. The biblical doctrine of creation maintains that God created all things, physical as well as spiritual. As a result, all things belong to him. He is able to use whatever he has made as a vehicle to communicate his goodness to us. In turn, the incarnation of Christ tells us that the eternal Word assumed human nature, body and soul. Our humanity has been taken into permanent union with the second person of the holy Trinity. The physical has been created by God and, in Christ, taken into union with him. Moreover, our salvation is not complete until our bodies are raised at the last day. Consistently throughout, physical and spiritual go together. To separate them in the way this view does is to render asunder what God has united.

Again, this interpretation has been fostered by the rise of individualism in the West. Since the Enlightenment, the individual has sprung to the foreground in contrast to the community. Descartes' philosophy (so influential in the development of modern Western culture), in seeking to establish the existence of God and the self from a position of radical systemic doubt, took its starting point from the phrase "I think, therefore I am." As a result, the existence of the thinking individual became the axiomatic basis of Western thought and culture. Its effect on the church and Christian thought has been immense. The evangelical movement of the eighteenth century focused on individual personal salvation and sanctification, while the church and sacraments were pushed into the background as secondary.[12] In turn, the Lord's Supper was removed from the context of the conveyance of grace and put in the position of being a private, individual matter in which the pious would contemplate the sufferings of the Savior.

In short, the popular idea of the Lord's Supper as a memorial only—the doctrine of the real absence of Christ—fails to do justice to the nature of the sacrament on exegetical, philosophical, and theological grounds.

Real Spiritual Presence: Communion

The classic Reformed view of the Lord's Supper as espoused by John Calvin and the documents of the Westminster Assembly joins the advocates of memorialism in rejecting a physical presence of Christ in the eucharist. For him to be human entails his being restricted physically to one place at one time. He cannot be ubiquitous according to his human nature without ceasing to be human. Indeed, if this were so we could hardly be saved since we need a human Christ to save us, a second Adam to undo the damage caused by the first.[13]

On the other hand, this viewpoint differs markedly from memorialism in claiming that Christ is indeed present in his Supper. More is involved than a remembrance on the part of the participants. In terms of the Gospel of John, Christ gives himself to be eaten and drunk in faith. This eating and drinking is not physical but is nonetheless real and true. Christ does not come down to us in his body and blood. Instead, we are lifted up to him by the Holy Spirit. Christ, being the eternal Son of God, is of course everywhere. Moreover, he has permanently united himself to the human nature assumed in the incarnation. In that sense, the person of Christ is present with us as we eat and drink. Yet, on earth, the Son of God was not restricted or confined to the humanity he assumed, but was simultaneously filling all things, directing the universe even as (according to the flesh) he walked the dusty roads of Palestine.[14] So, at the right hand of God, the Son fills and directs the universe (Col. 1:15–20), now unbreakably united to his assumed humanity, while in terms of that same humanity he is limited and in one place. Yet that humanity is never separate or apart from the divinity, the eternal Son of God with whom and in whom it is one undivided person. Thus, in the sacrament the Holy Spirit unites the faithful to the person of Christ as they eat and drink the signs, the physical elements of bread and wine. There is an inseparable conjunction of sign and reality. As truly as we eat the bread and drink the wine, so we feed on Christ by faith.

Hence, there is both a real, objective communion in the Lord's Supper and, at the same time, the condition of those who receive it is not incidental or superfluous. We feed on Christ through faith, as he taught. Faith does not exist apart from the Supper, but neither does the Supper apart from faith, for faith is indispensable. Just as we need a mouth to receive bread and wine, so we need faith to receive Christ. As Robert Bruce put it, "As soon as you receive the bread in your mouth (if you are a faithful man or woman) you receive the body of Christ in your soul, and that by faith." He goes on to underline that what we receive is first and foremost not the benefits of Christ, nor the graces that flow out of Christ, but Christ himself.[15] The role of those who take the sacrament is, therefore, to be believing and receptive. The physical and the spiritual are not merged (as in transubstantiation) nor are they separated (as in memorialism). Instead they are distinct but without separation. The physical can be the channel of grace, since God created all things, Christ assumed our human flesh, and our bodies will be raised (like his) at the last day.

THE LORD'S SUPPER IN REFORMED THEOLOGY

W hen you are at the Lord's Table, watching what the Minister does outwardly, in breaking and distributing the bread, in pouring out and distributing the wine, think of this: Christ is as busy doing all these things spiritually to your soul. He is busy giving to you His own body, with His own hand; He is as busy giving to you His own blood, with its power and efficacy. Likewise, in this action, if you are a faithful Communicant, think of what the mouth does, and how the mouth of the body is occupied outwardly; in the same way, the hand and mouth of the soul, which is faith, are occupied inwardly.[1]

We now turn to examine how early Reformed theology considered the Lord's Supper. The branch of the Reformed church centered on Zürich and led by Zwingli and his successor Heinrich Bullinger (1504–75) tended to consider the eucharist to be simply a memorial. However, the rest of the Reformed churches showed a broad measure of agreement, as expressed in classic confessions like the French Confession (1559), the Scots Confession (1560), the Belgic Confession (1561), and the Heidelberg Cathechism (1563).[2] We will focus our attention on the teaching of John Calvin, and then examine in detail the statements of the Westminster Assembly (1643–49).

John Calvin

Calvin's teaching on the Lord's Supper is found in his *Institutes* 4.17 and in his *Short Treatise on the Holy Supper of our Lord and only Saviour Jesus Christ*. In addition, he has some important comments in his *Commentary on the Epistle to the Ephesians*, in his remarks on chapter 5. Calvin also drew up a statement on the Supper with Heinrich Bullinger in 1549, the *Consensus Tigurinus*. This was a compromise document, designed to present a united front by the Swiss Reformed churches following the Augsburg Interim of 1548 that parceled up Europe between Roman Catholic and Lutheran jurisdictions. It is not an accurate portrayal of Calvin's own position, as is clear when comparing it with his *Short Treatise*.[3]

Calvin begins the chapter in the *Institutes* by arguing that the Lord's Supper provides the faithful with spiritual food, consisting in union with Christ who is present in the sacrament. It is "as if Christ here present were himself set before our eyes and touched with our hands."[4] God's promises are sealed as we are made partakers of Christ's flesh, a mystery more to be felt than explained. By true partaking of him, "his life passes into us and is made ours—just as bread when taken as food imparts vigor to the body."[5] This is a high and incomprehensible mystery.[6]

There are three major purposes for which the Lord gave this

sacrament. First, it serves to sign and seal in our consciences the promises of the gospel and to give us assurance that this is our true spiritual nourishment. As a result, we will have a right assurance of salvation. Second, it arouses us to praise him for his great goodness toward us. Third, it exhorts us to sanctity and brotherly love.[7] In doing this, it directs us emphatically to the cross and resurrection of Jesus Christ, for it is he who is the sum and substance of the whole sacrament.[8]

Since Christ is the sum of his Supper, the true communication of Christ is vital to understand. To deny this reality "is to render this holy sacrament frivolous and useless" and to commit "a blasphemy execrable and unworthy of attention." It is not only a matter of partaking of his Spirit; it is necessary also to partake of his humanity, for when he gives himself to us, he gives himself so that we possess him entirely. The bread and wine are signs, but the name and title of the body and blood are attributed to them since they are instruments by which Jesus Christ distributes them to us. Although this communion is incomprehensible, it is nevertheless visibly shown to us, just as the Holy Spirit took the form of a dove at Jesus' baptism.

> It is like this with the communion which we have with the body and blood of our Lord. It is a spiritual mystery, which cannot be seen by the eye, nor comprehended by the human understanding. It is therefore symbolized by visible signs . . . but in such a way that it is not a bare figure, but joined to its reality and substance. It is therefore with good reason that the bread is called body, since not only does it represent it to us, but also presents it to us . . . the sacraments of the Lord ought not and cannot at all be separated from their reality and substance. To distinguish them so that they be not confused is not only

good and reasonable but wholly necessary. But to divide them so as to set them up the one without the other is absurd.[9]

In his Ephesians commentary Calvin develops this further. He claims that "if we are to be true members of Christ we grow into one body by the communication of his substance" and that Paul is describing "our union to Christ, a symbol and pledge of which is given to us in the holy Supper." While some do not admit such a communication,

> Paul declares that we are of the members and bones of Christ. Do we wonder, then, if in the Supper He offers His body to be enjoyed by us, to nourish us unto eternal life? . . . Such is the union between us and Christ, that in a sense he pours himself into us. For we are not bone of His bone, and flesh of His flesh, because, like ourselves, He is man, but because, by the power of His Spirit, He engrafts us into His Body, so that from Him we derive life. . . . He concludes with wonder at the union between Christ and the Church. For he exclaims that this is a great mystery. By which he implies that no language can do it justice. . . .When they deny that the flesh and blood of Christ are offered to us in the Lord's Supper . . . I am overwhelmed with the depth of this mystery, and with Paul am not ashamed to acknowledge in wonder my ignorance. . . . Let us therefore labour more to feel Christ living in us, than to discover the nature of that communication.[10]

These statements of Calvin's demonstrate his grasp of the reality of Christ's communication of himself to the faithful and his appreciation of the emptiness of a memorialist understanding. When he speaks of this communication as spiritual, he explains that this is due to its origination by the Holy Spirit. The Spirit is the bond who unites us with Christ. It is therefore a real and true communication of Christ's body and blood and is spiritual since the Holy Spirit effects it.[11] Calvin was followed in this by others, such as Bucer and Vermigli; Robert Bruce, who was also not afraid to call the eucharist "a high and divine mystery"; and Amandus Polanus of Basel and Guilielmus Bucanus of Lausanne, both of whom agree that the faithful have communion with the body and blood of Christ in the Supper.[12]

Calvin also distances himself both from Luther and, hardly surprisingly, from Rome. The Roman Catholic doctrine of the Mass has brought a legion of errors that have corrupted and effectively destroyed the sacrament. At root are the ideas of the eucharist as a sacrifice and, following that, the dogma of transubstantiation. From these, all other idolatries and superstitions follow. Included in Calvin's denunciations are the adoration of the host, the reservation of the bread, keeping the cup from the people (which he likens to theft), and the absence of the Word, which is what makes the sacrament in the first place. This the Roman church has lost by reason of its plethora of false doctrines.[13]

Luther also comes in for extensive criticism, particularly over the crucial doctrine of the ubiquity of Christ's body which, Calvin contends, is in heaven. We must take into account the meaning and significance of the ascension. Since Christ has gone up to the right hand of God, he cannot, according to his humanity, be physically present here.[14] As a consequence, in the Lord's Supper, Christ is not brought down to us, but we are lifted up to him. The Lutherans have left nothing to the Holy Spirit. But it is the Spirit who unites Christ to us.

To them Christ does not seem present unless he comes
down to us. As though, if he should lift us to himself, we
should not just as much enjoy his presence! The question is therefore only of the manner, for they place
Christ in the bread, while we do not think it lawful for
us to drag him from heaven.[15]

Calvin also differs from Westphal's teaching on the mixing of
Christ's flesh with the human soul. Instead, he says, Christ
"breathes life into our souls . . . indeed, pours his very life into
us," even though his actual flesh does not enter into us.[16] This
flows from Calvin's rejection of a physical communion. Westphal, and other more extreme Lutherans, do wrong to the Holy
Spirit, he says. It is through his incomprehensible power that we
are enabled to share in Christ's flesh and blood. This is a mystery
not reducible to a corporal eating.[17]

How are we to use the Lord's Supper, and in what manner
should we come to it? Calvin stresses the grave danger of contempt
for, or indifference toward, the sacrament. This is to misuse it and
to contaminate it—an intolerable sacrilege against what God has
sanctified.[18] Instead, we are to examine ourselves to see whether
we have repentance and faith. We must hold firm that Jesus Christ
is our sole righteousness. Of ourselves we are weak and miserable,
but he is strong and gracious.[19] The eucharist also brings responsi-
bilities concerning our conduct and attitude toward other people.
Before partaking, we must not bear hatred toward anyone, for this
is a sacrament of reconciliation.[20] Again, this examination is
self-examination and does not justify our acting in judgment on
others who may be about to receive communion. We have no right
to pass judgment on them. That is a matter belonging to the proper
ecclesiastical authorities. Excommunication can only take place
when notorious sin is proved by proper ecclesiastical judgment.

It is not the office of each individual to judge and discriminate, in order to admit or reject as seems to him good; seeing that this prerogative belongs generally to the Church as a whole, or rather to the pastor with the elders whom he ought to have for assisting him in the government of the Church. For Paul does not command us to examine others, but each is to examine himself.[21]

On the other hand, this self-examination is not intended to convey the impression that only those who have attained perfection can receive the Lord's Supper. Faith and love are necessary on our part, not an unattainable perfection. If a perfect penitence and assurance were required, none of us could attend, for we would all be excluded.[22]

Calvin was convinced that the Lord's Supper should be held more frequently than was the custom in his day. While there was no detailed or binding requirement as to how often it should be observed, he was sure that it should be "as frequently as the capacity of the people will allow."[23] In the church of Rome, the Mass was usually received very infrequently. The Fourth Lateran Council (1215) required it to be held once a year. As is well known, Calvin's own wish for Geneva was that it be celebrated on a weekly basis. However, the Council overruled his wishes and restricted it to once per month.

The Westminster Standards

We will examine the teaching of The Westminster Confession of Faith (WCF, 1647), chapter 29, and refer in passing to parallel statements in The Westminster Shorter Catechism (WSC) and The Westminster Larger Catechism (WLC). The position of the Assembly has often been taken for granted or ignored, with the result that important tracts of this chapter are virtually forgotten by those who claim allegiance to Presbyterian or Reformed doctrine.

> Our Lord Jesus, in the night wherein he was betrayed, instituted the sacrament of his body and blood, called the Lord's Supper, to be observed in his church, unto the end of the world, for the perpetual remembrance of the sacrifice of himself in his death; the sealing all benefits thereof unto true believers, their spiritual nourishment and growth in him, their further engagement in and to all duties which they owe unto him; and, to be a bond and pledge of their communion with him, and with each other, as members of his mystical body. (WCF 29.1)

The first section recounts the founding of the Lord's Supper by Jesus and the purposes for which he gave it. There are five discernible reasons for it. First, it is a permanent memorial of his sacrificial death. We recall how this is an indisputable part of the sacrament, even though it is not the only part.

The second purpose is "the sealing all benefits thereof [of his death] unto true believers." The benefits of Christ's death encompass the whole of redemption. The previous chapters in the Confession have listed the fruits of Christ's passion. Included are effectual calling, justification, adoption, sanctification, saving faith, repentance, good works, perseverance, and assurance (chapters 10–18). The Lord's Supper functions as a seal of these benefits, affirming them and assuring us of their truth and reality. (In the 1640s a seal was something that authenticated or confirmed something, or attested a promise, often of a covenant.)[24]

Third, the Supper provides for "their [true believers'] spiritual nourishment and growth in him." Entailed here is feeding and sustenance akin to the physical feeding that sustains our bodily lives. Not only is the Supper the occasion of our succor, but it also enables us to grow in union with Christ.

Fourth, it engages true believers "in and to all duties which they owe unto him." It impels us to obedience. On the one hand, the focus on the love of Christ, seen in his freely giving himself to the cross, acts, under the direction of the Holy Spirit, as a powerful impetus to drive us on to follow him more faithfully. At the same time, the nourishment and consequent growth in Christ that we enjoy elicits an answering response on our part, given by the Holy Spirit, of thankful love and willing obedience.

Fifth, it is for true believers "a bond and pledge of their communion with him, and with each other, as members of his mystical body." Here the Confession points further toward union and communion with Christ, at the same time stressing that this union also has inseparable horizontal connections too. We have communion with Christ, and *at the same time and as a direct corollary,* communion with the body of Christ here on earth. Head and members are indissolubly united. The Confession holds back here from the full expansiveness of Calvin, and it is not until section 7 that it approaches the point he reached. Nevertheless, all the ingredients are present here for the full-orbed Reformed teaching.

> In this sacrament, Christ is not offered up to his Father; nor any real sacrifice made at all, for remission of sins of the quick or the dead; but only a commemoration of that one offering up of himself, by himself, upon the cross, once for all: and a spiritual oblation of all possible praise unto God, for the same: so that the popish sacrifice of the mass (as they call it) is most abominably injurious to

Christ's one, only sacrifice, the alone propitiation for all
the sins of his elect. (29.2)

The Confession here targets the Church of Rome. It distances itself radically from the dogma of the Mass. In particular,
the priestly view of the church and its ministry that underlay Roman Catholic sacramentalism receives short shrift. "Christ is not
offered up to his Father; nor any real sacrifice made"—in short,
the minister is not a priest and the Supper is not a sacrifice.
Christ's offering is neither extended, repeated, or prolonged. It
was once-for-all, since it was perfect and complete for our redemption. Thus in this sense the Supper is a memorial of a com-
pleted act, an act that took place "upon the cross, once for all."
We are reminded here of the wonderful statement in Article 31
of The Thirty-Nine Articles of the Church of England (1563,
1571), which document the Assembly was charged with revising:
"The offering of Christ once made is that perfect redemption,
propitiation and satisfaction . . . and there is none other satisfaction for man, but that alone."[25]

On the other hand, the Lord's Supper *is* a sacrifice of a kind—
a spiritual sacrifice of praise to God, as Hebrews puts it in
13:15–16. We might even say ourselves that the reality on which it
is founded is the one sacrifice of Christ on the cross and so, in
communion with him, we share in that perfect sacrifice. The
problem with the Roman position lies in the sacrificial view of
church and ministry and the consequent implication (even if official dogma tried hard to maintain the once-for-all nature of the
cross)[26] of a priestly, bloodless repetition. The outcome, the Confession states, is injurious to the perception of the work of Christ—
exceedingly injurious, abominably injurious. The Confession can
have no truck with the Mass but both here, and later, its statements, while strong, are measured and have a certain restraint.

> The Lord Jesus hath, in this ordinance, appointed his
> ministers to declare his word of institution to the people;
> to pray, and bless the elements of bread and wine, and
> thereby to set them apart from a common to an holy use;
> and to take and break the bread, to take the cup, and
> (they communicating also themselves) to give both to
> the communicants; but to none who are not then pres-
> ent in the congregation. (29.3)

Here is spelled out the task of the minister and what he actually does. The minister is given this role by the Lord Jesus himself, and so he is appointed by the Lord whose Supper it is and
who has exclusive rights to determine what may and may not be
done. He has appointed ministers and no one else to administer
the sacraments (see 27.4) because the Word governs the sacrament and thus a minister of the Word alone is authorized to pre-
side. Thus, the very first thing—the matter of the utmost
importance—is that they "declare his word of institution to the
people." This makes the sacrament—it is a necessary condition
for the Lord's Supper to be. Without a minister declaring the
word of institution, there is no sacrament. Entailed in this is that
private instances of the eucharist in which a loose aggregation of
believers participate without "a minister of the Word lawfully ordained" are not instances of the Lord's Supper at all.

Second, the minister is "to pray, and bless the elements of
bread and wine." Note, he does not effect a change of substance.
They remain bread and wine. On the other hand, they are now
set apart to a holy use. While we must not worship them and
have no need to reserve them, we should still treat them re-
spectfully and dispose of them appropriately, for they have been
dedicated to a sacred purpose. We recall here that the giving of
thanks at this point gives to the Supper the name of eucharist. In

41

addition, we note that the elements the Lord Jesus appointed are "bread and wine" and that the right to determine these rests with him alone, and not with the temperance movement of the nineteenth century. While Jesus changed the water into wine, the temperance movement changed the wine into grape juice concentrate. No one has any right to change the elements of the Lord's Supper, any more than in baptism they can replace water by orange juice. To do this is to usurp the authority of Christ.

Third, the minister is "to take and break the bread" in the sight of the people. This entails a single loaf, in conformity with the practice of the early church (1 Cor. 10:16–17). The first name for the sacrament was "the breaking of bread." Here is why Augustine could call the sacrament a "visible word of God," for the breaking of the bread graphically portrays the breaking of Christ's body on the cross to deliver us from sin. The fraction (breaking of the bread) thus takes place in the sight of the people, not behind closed doors where it is visible to no one.

Fourth and similarly, the minister takes the cup. Again, there is to be one cup, just as there is one loaf. The church is one body, for Christ is not divided into one hundred or more fragments. The minister gives the cup to the laity, unlike Rome, for there is no fear in Protestantism of the blood of Christ spilling on the ground since the wine remains simply wine.

Finally, the Confession warns against private instances of the Lord's Supper. This is a sacrament of the church, the body of Christ. It is decisively *not* to be understood as an individual, private, spiritual experience. It is not to be observed by a group of laypeople traveling home in a coach from a ski trip. It is corporate first, and individual only within that clearly understood and defined context.[27]

Private masses, or receiving this sacrament by a priest, or any other, alone; as likewise, the denial of the cup to the people, worshiping the elements, the lifting them up, or carrying them about, for adoration, and the reserving them for any pretended religious use; are all contrary to the nature of this sacrament, and to the institution of Christ. (29.4)

This section reinforces the teaching of the last. The errors of Rome receive further assault. Private Masses, the denial of the cup to the laity, the worshiping and reserving of the elements are all contrary to the sacrament and Christ's institution. All these are due to the fundamental error of transubstantiation. If that were true, these should follow, and so they do. This may explain the balanced and judicious attack on Rome. These are contrary to what Christ commanded. But the language of the Confession is restrained. We may add a rider. When the Confession opposes the lifting up of the elements, it does so *because of the worship that follows*—"the lifting them up, or carrying them about, for adoration." The veneration of the host is the point at issue, flowing from the change of substance that Rome considers to take place. It is this latter point (the change of substance) that is the source of the problem. The Confession does not oppose lifting the elements *so that the people may see them*, for this is an essential part of the sacrament as Christ appointed it.

The outward elements in this sacrament, duly set apart to the uses ordained by Christ, have such relation to him crucified, as that, truly, yet sacramentally only, they are sometimes called by the name of the things they represent, to wit, the body and blood of Christ; albeit, in sub-

stance and nature, they still remain truly and only bread
and wine, as they were before. (29.5)

This section considers the relation between the signs and
the reality. Once consecrated, the bread and wine have an exceedingly close relation to Christ. They remain bread and
wine and do not change their substance. Nevertheless, due to
the sacramental relation, they can be called the body and
blood of Christ.

> That doctrine which maintains a change of the sub-
> stance of bread and wine, into the substance of Christ's
> body and blood (commonly called transubstantiation)
> by consecration of a priest, or by any other way, is re-
> pugnant, not to Scripture alone, but even to common
> sense, and reason; overthroweth the nature of the sacra-
> ment, and hath been, and is, the cause of manifold su-
> perstitions; yea, of gross idolatries. (29.6)

At last the Confession gets to grips with the root of its opposition to the Roman Catholic doctrine, the teaching on transubstantiation. It is repugnant not only to Scripture but to reason
and common sense. It overthrows the sacrament. We saw how
the Confession regarded it as "abominably injurious" to the one
sacrifice of Christ. Transubstantiation itself is "the cause of man-
ifold superstitions; yea, of gross idolatries." The point is that these
superstitions, idolatries, and injuries *result from* transubstantiation. The Assembly sees that this is the root problem and that the
superstitions flow from here. Once this dogma is accepted, idolatries follow. Thus the real problem is the dogma. The way the
Confession deals with it is to point to its departure from Scripture and to indicate that it is rationally insupportable.

> Worthy receivers, outwardly partaking of the visible ele-
> ments, in this sacrament, do then also, inwardly by faith,
> really and indeed, yet not carnally and corporally but
> spiritually, receive, and feed upon, Christ crucified, and
> all the benefits of his death: the body and blood of Christ
> being then, not corporally or carnally, in, with, or under
> the bread and wine; yet, as really, but spiritually, present
> to the faith of believers in that ordinance, as the ele-
> ments themselves are to their outward senses. (29.7)

This, to my mind, is the single most significant part of the
chapter and the one most neglected. It speaks of what happens
in the Lord's Supper when "worthy receivers" or true believers
receive the outward elements. It is full of negative statements dis-
tancing it from the Lutheran teaching and encumbered by a suc-
cession of clauses piled on top of one another. The entire section
is, in fact, only one sentence.

First, we note the negatives. The Confession deals less vehemently with the Lutheran doctrine since it is less injurious
than the Roman Catholic. However, the Lutheran teaching is
clearly opposed. True believers do not feed on Christ "carnally
and corporally," for the body and blood of Christ are not "corporally or carnally, in, with, or under the bread and wine." Con-
substantiation is rejected. Christ is not present physically. It is
important to see what this section rejects so we can detach it
from the convoluted language and then move on to see what
the Confession affirms.

Second, the positive affirmation is clear. True believers "inwardly, by faith, really and indeed, . . . spiritually, receive, and
feed upon, Christ crucified, and all the benefits of his death."
The reason for this is that "the body and blood of Christ being
. . . as really, but spiritually, present to the faith of believers . . .

as the elements themselves are to the outward senses." The main coordinate verbs of the whole are "receive" and "feed upon." True believers receive and feed upon Christ, as surely as they eat the outward elements. Christ is the key, for this is *the Lord's* Supper. This section teaches the same as Calvin: that there is a true feeding on Christ in the eucharist, not after a physical manner, but by the Holy Spirit. This is a real and a true feeding, a communion that sustains and nourishes us and so brings about our growth in union with Christ.

> Although ignorant and wicked men receive the outward elements in this sacrament; yet, they receive not the thing signified thereby; but, by their unworthy coming thereunto, are guilty of the body and blood of the Lord, to their own damnation. Wherefore, all ignorant and ungodly persons, as they are unfit to enjoy communion with him, so are they unworthy of the Lord's table; and cannot, without great sin against Christ, while they remain such, partake of these holy mysteries, or be admitted thereunto. (29.8)

The final section of the chapter discusses who may receive the Lord's Supper. First of all, it distinguishes between those who receive the elements and those who receive Christ. It is, sadly, possible to eat and drink bread and wine only. Since transubstantiation is rejected, it is possible to have the sign but not the reality. Since faith is necessary to feed on Christ (here are echoes of John 6), those without faith or godliness do not receive Christ at all, even though they may receive the sacrament. Moreover, they are guilty of the body and blood of Christ and so liable to damnation. They sin against Christ by participating. They cannot be admitted to the table.

These people are described as "ignorant" and "wicked." This implies that knowledge and piety are necessary. True believers or worthy receivers are those with faith, and who are able to examine themselves concerning their knowledge, faith, and repentance (WSC 97). Those "who are found to be ignorant and scandalous," whom the church authorities may after due process have determined to lack saving faith or to be living an ungodly life, are to be kept from the Lord's Supper (WLC 174). Since the Confession and Catechisms all regard baptism as the sacrament of initiation, coming before the Lord's Supper, a strong implication is that any who have not been baptized lack the knowledge requisite for participation too.

> What food luxurious loads the board,
> when at his table sits the Lord!
> The wine how rich, the bread how sweet,
> when Jesus deigns the guests to meet!
>
> If now with eyes defiled and dim,
> we see the signs, but see not him;
> O may his love the scales displace,
> and bid us see him face to face!
>
> O glorious Bridegroom of our hearts,
> your present smile a heav'n imparts!
> O lift the veil, if veil there be,
> let every saint your glory see.
>
> C. H. Spurgeon (1834–92)

THE LORD'S SUPPER IN PRACTICE

We have already encountered the close connection between the Word of God and the sacraments. The two go together and, between them, the Word has priority in both its written and preached form. This is so for two reasons.

First, we must recognize the status of the Word of God in itself. The Bible is the speech of God, breathed out by God (2 Tim. 3:16), the product of the Holy Spirit sweeping the human authors along in a mighty current so that their own human discourse was, at the same time, the speech of God (2 Peter 1:20–21). Behind this is the ministry of the ascended Christ, who received the promise of the Holy Spirit from the Father.[1] Again, the proclamation of the Word of God "by ministers of the gospel lawfully called"[2] is to be received as the Word of God himself. Paul refers to Christ preaching through preachers of the gospel (Rom. 1:14; Eph. 2:17).[3] We should note here too that there is a living, dynamic connection among the eternal Word, the written Word (Scripture), and preaching.[4] Thus, the reading and preaching of

49

Holy Scripture share, by the grace of God, in the utter priority of the address of God to us in the gospel.

Second, it is the Word that creates the sacraments. This is true on a number of levels. First, the incarnate Word, Jesus Christ, appointed both baptism and the eucharist to be continued in his church throughout the age. Thus, he has full authority over them. Second, Jesus did this by means of his spoken Word, recorded for us in the Bible. Thus the written Word defines and describes them for us. Third, as signs they point beyond themselves to the transcendent reality with which they are connected. This connection and significance requires explanation, or the sacramental ritual is reduced simply to a bare ritual. Therefore, the Word (read and preached) must always go with sacrament.

In consequence, since the Word has priority, the sacraments must always be administered by a minister of the Word properly ordained. Ordination sets a man apart for the task of ministering the Word of God. As the church ordains, so too does the Holy Spirit (Acts 13:1–7). Without the preaching of the Word by one lawfully called, there is no sacrament.[5]

Elements of the Lord's Supper

A Single Loaf

It is clear that the Lord's Supper as practiced in the New Testament church used a single loaf. So much is evident from the earliest description of the Supper as "the breaking of bread." Paul, too, comments on the church at the eucharist being "one loaf" (1 Cor. 10:16–17). This gives eloquent witness to two vital things. First, it vividly portrays the body of Christ being broken for us on the cross. The tearing apart of the loaf depicts the violent and dreadful death by which we have been delivered from sin and condemnation. Second, it demonstrates that all the faithful share in the one body of Christ. As each removes a segment from a broken piece of the one loaf, the message is visibly conveyed that "because there is one loaf, we, who are many, are one body, for we all partake of the one loaf" (1 Cor. 10:17). On the one hand, we all share in Christ and have fellowship or communion with his body and blood. On the other hand, we all share in the unity of the body of Christ, the church.

The practice, very common in many churches, of presenting bread pre-cut into dozens or hundreds of tiny bite-sized pieces misses this entirely. Instead, it is redolent of post-Enlightenment individualism, where religion is conceived of as a private, inward matter between the individual soul and God. This is to change the sacrament, indeed to violate and pollute it. Augustine's comment on the eucharist as a "visible word of God" loses its sense. The element of proclaiming Christ's death, mentioned by Paul in 1 Corinthians 11, is blurred. Besides, we noted how the Westminster Assembly lists the tasks of the minister to include taking and breaking the bread in the sight of the people. For churches in the Presbyterian tradition to employ pre-cut bread is a departure from their confessional standards and from the intent of the eucharist.[6]

A Single Cup

Many of the arguments against pre-cut bread apply also to the common practice today of individual plastic cups. Here again is the triumph of individualism. Both the New Testament and the Westminster Standards refer to "the cup" in the singular. The Confession 29.3 explicitly says that the minister is to "take the cup" in the presence of the people, at the same occasion as he reads the words of institution, gives thanks, and breaks the bread. As with the single loaf, the visibility of these words of God is maintained by holding to this important principle and is correspondingly diminished by departing from it. In both cases, concerns for hygiene (misplaced, since there is no recorded instance of worse health among the vast majority of Christians who have always used a single cup) have taken precedence over the intention of our Lord. This should not be, for it is his sacrament.

> It is clear then that no man or creature has power to make a Sacrament; therefore it must be according to the institution of Christ. Consider what He said, what He did, and what He commanded you to do: all that must be said, done and obeyed. It is His intention that must be kept. If you leave undone one jot of what He commanded you to do, you pervert the institution, for there is nothing in the register of the institution but what is essential . . . if we leave any particular point or ceremony belonging to this institution undone, we pervert the whole action.[7]

Wine

The use of wine in the eucharist is not mentioned specifically in the New Testament. However, down through the centuries it has been the uniform practice. However, there was no reason why it should have been mentioned. Wine was the regular, everyday drink (not only at Passover), as it still is to this day throughout the Mediterranean world. Even an unfermented juice from the grape will quickly ferment in that climate.

Only with the rise of the temperance movement in the nineteenth century was an aversion to alcohol allowed to intrude into the Christian church. Many capitulated to this militant movement. While the Bible condemns drunkenness as a sin (Deut. 21:20; Prov. 3:20–21; 1 Cor. 6:10), it consistently speaks favor-

ably of wine. Wine is a gift of God (as a random sample: Gen.
14:18; 27:28, 37; Lev. 23:13; Pss. 4:7; 104:15; Prov. 3:10 et al.)
that gladdens the heart of man. The eschatological feast will con-
sist inter alia of the best wine (Isa. 25:1–8). For his first miracle,
Jesus, in affirming the creation ordinance of marriage, changed
water into wine. In doing so he signified that he would surpass
the provisions of the Old Testament (John 2:1–11).[8] The temperance movement's disapproval of wine is alien to Scripture
and both meaningless and irrelevant to a culture one of whose
three main agricultural activities was viniculture.

Wine itself conveys the intoxicating nature of the gospel.
Feeding on Christ is the most enjoyable thing that could be
done. It is the heart of the Christian faith, gladdening the heart
of the faithful.

Unleavened Bread?

To be true to our confessional standards and to Scripture,
should we not use unleavened bread in the Lord's Supper as Jesus must have done at the Last Supper, following the practice of
the Passover?

First, is the Lord's Supper a direct successor to the Passover,
as is often supposed? This has been widely accepted ever since
the late–fourth-century document the *Apostolic Constitutions*
was found in the seventh century. However, scholarship has concluded that this work read later beliefs into earlier writers and
that hard historical evidence for many dogmatically held beliefs
about primitive Christian practice is lacking. In 1981 Geoffrey
Cuming concluded concerning early eucharistic liturgies that
"the time has come to rewrite the textbooks."[9] In fact, it is far
more likely that we should understand communion in the light
of the sacrificial covenantal meal in Exodus 24, when Moses and
Aaron, Nadab and Abihu, and seventy elders of Israel climbed

the mountain, saw God, and ate and drank immediately after Moses had sprinkled the people with the blood of the covenant.[10] As Paul Bradshaw writes, "From the point of view of liturgical scholars, the question of whether the Last Supper was a Passover meal is not particularly crucial. Even if it *were* a Passover meal, no exclusively paschal practices seem to have been retained in the primitive Church's eucharistic celebrations."[11]

Following this, the evidence (such as we have) indicates the church in the early centuries universally used ordinary leavened bread. By the eighth century, the bread and wine had officially begun to be identified with the body and blood of Christ. Since leavened bread was more likely to crumble and so fragment the body of Christ, Rome required the use of unleavened bread. However, the East refused to follow, accusing Rome of Judaizing tendencies, and to this day it continues to use ordinary leavened bread.

The New Testament terminology is important. The word for unleavened bread (*azymos*) is used to refer to the Feast of Un-leavened Bread, coinciding with the Passover. However, the word consistently used in connection with the Lord's Supper is the wider ranging term *artos*, meaning a small round loaf of or-dinary bread. This is the word ascribed to Jesus in the Gospel ac-counts and, indeed, is the only word used for the bread in the Lord's Supper.

A. A. Hodge, in response to the question "What kind of bread is to be used in the sacrament . . . ?" argues that this is not specified, nor rendered essential by the nature of the service. "Christ used unleavened bread because it was present at the Passover. The early Christians celebrated the Communion at a common meal, with the bread of common life, which was leav-ened."[12] Calvin also considered "whether the bread is leavened or unleavened; the wine red or white—it makes no difference."[13]

As such, the question of leavened or unleavened bread is of the same order as whether we should use burgundy or port. What is clear is that the elements to be used in the Last Supper are bread and wine ("the fermented juice of the grape . . . that wine and no other liquid is to be used is clear from the record of the institution");[14] but as to the exact brand of bread or wine we have no precise requirement.

Paedo-Communion?

In recent years a growing number of people have advocated paedo-communion—giving communion to infants and very young children who have not made a public profession of faith. Two factors have encouraged this. One is a new interest in Eastern Orthodoxy, for the East has always practiced paedo-communion.[15] With the reemergence of the Eastern churches into the consciousness of the West, this practice has come into the spotlight. Another influence is a revived focus on covenant theology. Some have thought, assuming the eucharist fulfills the Passover, that if the whole family participated in the Passover and continues to do so in baptism, why should the Lord's Supper be kept from the entire household? Possibly the home-school movement has encouraged this focus.

Paedo-communion is opposed presciently in The Westminster Larger Catechism (177).[16] It seems to fit best with one of two positions on the eucharist that are vehemently opposed by the Reformed churches.

The first good fit for paedo-communion is transubstantiation. If there is a change of substance and the bread becomes the body of Christ, then it follows that whoever eats the bread receives the body of Christ. Therefore, to deny the bread to infants is to deny them grace. Thus, on the terms of transubstantiation, opposition to paedo-communion is seriously wrong. The Eastern church believes in transubstantiation, although in a less developed sense than Rome. Rome itself has somehow seen that faith is necessary.

The other position compatible with paedo-communion is memorialism. If the Lord's Supper is simply a figurative remembrance and not a means of grace (and still less a means of judgment to the unbelieving), it can hardly matter who receives the Lord's Supper, since no adverse consequences are likely to ensue.

However, the Reformed and biblical view stresses that the Lord's Supper requires on the part of those who receive it faith, repentance, and self-examination. If the means of grace can become a means of judgment, discipline, and even damnation, it is essential that participants are duly qualified—as penitent sinners.[17] To sum up, all that we have seen of the nature of the eucharist leads us to oppose paedo-communion as resting on one of two serious errors, both of which empty the sacrament of its proper significance.

This reminds us that there are definite qualifications required for taking the Lord's Supper. First comes baptism, for this is the sacrament of initiation that by definition precedes the eucharist. Baptism is acceptable if administered in the triune name, whether by Roman Catholic, Orthodox, or Protestant. Second comes public profession of faith, since saving faith is essential to feed on Christ the bread of life. Because the eucharist is a sacrament of the church, not a matter of private or individual choice, this faith must be tested and examined by the officers of the church to detect, as far as is possible, its credibility. Third comes active membership in a church that holds to the historic Christian faith. The Bible defines a Christian as a part of Christ's church. There must be no free-wheeling individuals running independently of the church (cf. 1 John 3:11–5; 4:7–21).

Frequency of the Lord's Supper

The New Testament does not give us a binding statement as to how often the Lord's Supper should be held. To that extent, the church is at liberty to arrange it as frequently as it sees fit. One thing we do know, and that is the extent to which it was held in the primitive church as recorded in Acts. In Acts 2 it was a regular feature of church life. The disciples devoted themselves to "the breaking of bread." We saw earlier that the phrase is in an ecclesiastical context, linked with the apostles' teaching, fellowship, the prayers, and the temple. The church at Troas met each week for the express purpose "to break bread" (Acts 20:7). Again, at Corinth the regular purpose of church gatherings was to observe the Lord's Supper (1 Cor. 11:18ff.). However, while the example of the early church is a guide, it cannot bind us, any more than their disposal of personal property *requires* us to do likewise. However, in general the church has recognized that the Lord's Supper is to be a regular and frequent part of its life.

This recognition was certainly true at the time of the Reformation. Scottish Presbyterianism prior to the Westminster Assembly had a different hue than after the persecutions launched under Charles II. Its shape originated in Geneva and was brought to Scotland by Knox, who spent much of the Marian exile there. The service was led by a lay reader, the ancient creeds and the Lord's Prayer were used at every service, and the deacons were actively involved, as they were in the French and Dutch Reformed churches of the day. Moreover, the Lord's Supper was to be held frequently, "commonly . . . once a month or so oft as the Congregation shall think expedient."[18]

During the Reformation, in 1561, when John Knox was ministering to his congregation in Edinburgh, he once held communion services daily for a week.[19]

As for Calvin, in his *Short Treatise* (1540) he states,

> If we have careful regard to the end for which our Lord intended it, we should realise that the use of it ought to be more frequent than many make it. . . . Therefore the custom ought to be well established, in all churches, of celebrating the Supper as frequently as the capacity of the people will allow. . . . Though we have no express command defining the time and the day, it should be enough for us to know that the intention of our Lord is that we use it often; otherwise we shall not know well the benefits which it offers us.[20]

In his *Articles Concerning the Organization of the Church and of Worship in Geneva* (1541), proposed to the Council of Ministers of Geneva, Calvin argues that "it would be well to require that the Communion of the Holy Supper of Jesus Christ be held every Sunday at least as a rule."[21] Calvin was overruled by both the Little Council and the Council of Two Hundred.[22]

In England, Thomas Cranmer, the great reforming Archbishop of Canterbury who Diarmaid MacCulloch in his magisterial biography demonstrates had the goal of making the Church of England a thoroughly Reformed church,[23] produced a liturgy that held the allegiance of many Puritans. Cranmer insisted on frequent, at least weekly, communion. In the reform of ecclesiastical law he introduced in 1552, he clearly specified this. These sections, among many others, were editorialized in Cranmer's own handwriting. For instance, in the section "Concerning the Celebration of Divine Offices," chapter 3, fol. 70v, on the administration of Holy Communion on Sundays and Feast Days, he wrote, "On Sundays and the feasts of the churches which are called cathedrals we command that there be this order in the divine services . . . after the completion of morning prayers . . . let the communion follow." Again, in chapter 7, fol. 72r, v, on the taking of the Lord's Supper it is stated, "It will be common to all churches that, *unless some grave cause demands otherwise*, the Lord's Supper will be taken only on Sundays" (my italics, indicating a section in Cranmer's own handwriting). The previous day it was required that communicants gather with the minister to examine their consciences and explore their faith.[24]

While Presbyterianism became known for infrequent communions, the Westminster Assembly took a very different line. The Directory for the Public Worship of God specified that the Lord's Supper be held often.

> The communion, or supper of the Lord, is frequently to be celebrated; but how often, may be considered and determined by the ministers, and other church-governors of each congregation, as they shall find most convenient for the comfort and edification of the people committed to their charge.[25]

Scottish Presbyterians moved to infrequent communion by historical accident rather than design. After the Restoration in 1660, Charles II attempted to enforce the Royal Supremacy over the Scottish kirk. Many dissented. The Covenanters took to arms. Many ministers were imprisoned or martyred. Persecuted congregations were often forced to meet in secret. Ministers were in short supply. As a matter of necessity, communion could be held only every so often, when a minister happened to be in the area. By the time religious liberty was granted, with the accession of William of Orange and Mary in 1688, infrequent communion had become part of the tradition. However, in the beginning it was not so.

The bottom line on frequency is that the church is free to hold the Lord's Supper as often as it deems appropriate. There is no binding requirement. However, the degree to which the church desires it is a reliable gauge of how eagerly it wants Christ. An old argument against frequent communion (familiarity breeds contempt) deserves short shrift. Does that apply too to prayer, Scripture reading, preaching, or your relationship with your spouse? Does it even apply to Christ? While it remains a matter of Christian liberty, the key word is "often." The question to ask ourselves is simply this: How much do we hunger and thirst for righteousness? How far do we desire communion with Christ? As Robert Bruce put it so vividly, "If Christ is not both eaten and digested, He can do us no good, but this digestion cannot exist where there is not a greedy appetite to receive Him."[26]

Thou art the everlasting Word,
the Father's only Son;
God manifestly seen and heard,
and heaven's belovèd one.
Worthy, O Lamb of God, art thou
that every knee to thee should bow.

Throughout the universe of bliss,
the centre thou, and sun;
the eternal theme of praise is this,
to heaven's belovèd one.
Worthy, O Lamb of God, art thou
that every knee to thee should bow.

Josiah Conder (1789–1855)

THE LORD'S SUPPER
AND THE FUTURE

Come, let us join our cheerful songs
with angels round the throne.
Ten thousand thousand are their tongues
but all their joys are one.

"Worthy the Lamb that died," they cry,
"to be exalted thus."
"Worthy the Lamb," our lips reply,
"for he was slain for us."

Jesus is worthy to receive
honour and power divine
and blessings more than we can give
be Lord for ever thine

The whole creation join in one
to bless the sacred name

EPILOGUE

of him who sits upon the throne
and to adore the Lamb.

Isaac Watts (1674–1748)

When initiating the Supper, Jesus said, "I will not eat it
again until it finds fulfillment in the kingdom of God. . . . I will
not drink again of the fruit of the vine until the kingdom of God
comes" (Luke 22:16, 18). He was looking forward to the time of
fulfillment, the eschatological feast to which Isaiah alluded (Isa.
25:1–8). There, the relationship between Christ and his church
will be consummated. The central covenant promise, "I will be
your God, you shall be my people," will come to its ultimate
fruition. No longer will we "see through a glass darkly," for we
shall see face to face. The communion the church enjoys with
Christ will be unimpeded by sin.

However, in measure we have a foretaste of that great ban-
quet already. Christ promises to have supper with us here and
now (cf. Rev. 3:20). The author of the Letter to the Hebrews
points out that the church already has one foot in heaven. Warning against the danger of Hebrew believers reverting to some
form of idealistic Judaism by venerating the past, especially the
wilderness generation led by Moses, he says that New Testament
worship is, in essence, communion with the Triune God in fellowship with the entire church and joined with the whole an-
gelic throng.

> You have not come to a mountain that might be touched
> and that is burning with fire; to darkness, gloom and
> storm; to a trumpet blast or to such a voice speaking
> words that those who heard it begged that no further
> word be spoken to them, because they could not bear

what was commanded: "If even an animal touches the mountain, it must be stoned." The sight was so terrifying that Moses said, "I am trembling with fear."

But you have come to Mount Zion, to the heavenly Jerusalem, the city of the living God. You have come to thousands upon thousands of angels in joyful assembly, to the church of the first-born, whose names are written in heaven. You have come to God, the judge of all men, to the spirits of righteous men made perfect, to Jesus the mediator of a new covenant, and to the sprinkled blood that speaks a better word than the blood of Abel.

The church's worship is therefore communion with the risen Christ, in company with the angels and the church in heaven. The fourth and fifth chapters of Revelation present a picture of this scene. While we are engrossed in our everyday affairs, feet firmly planted on the ground, we are simultaneously lifted up to heaven by the Holy Spirit to participate in the cosmic adoration of the redeemed in heaven, with other creatures joining in to add their voices as they look on. In the eucharist (the giving of thanks) this comes to focus. Preceded by the preached word—into which angels long to look (1 Peter 1:12)—the Lord's Supper draws us into ever closer union with him who is "the eternal theme of praise." The Lord's Supper and the Lamb's Supper are two sides of the same reality.

Therefore with angels and archangels and with all the company of heaven, we proclaim your great and glorious name, forever praising you and saying

Holy, holy, holy Lord,
God of power and might.

EPILOGUE

Heaven and earth are full of your glory.
Hosanna in the highest.[1]

In a context such as this, Thomas Aquinas had his famous auditory vision. In terms a Reformed Christian would suspect because of the heavy content of vision and merit, nevertheless its central theme shines forth and resonates down the centuries to believers of whatever stripe. There in the Priory Chapel at Naples, at the communion service, he heard Christ say to him, "You have written well of me, Thomas. What do you desire as a reward for your labours?" To which Thomas replied, "Lord, only yourself."[2]

That, surely, is the great theme of the Christian faith and the supreme focus of the Supper bequeathed us by Christ. What do we want from it? What do we seek above all else? "Lord, only yourself."

NOTES

Page viii Epigraph
Robert Bruce, *The Mystery of the Lord's Supper*, trans. and ed. Thomas F. Torrance (London: James Clarke, 1958), 39–40.

Introduction
1 John W. Nevin, "Doctrine of the Reformed Church on the Lord's Supper," *The Mercersburg Review* 2 (1850): 421–548. As Bard Thompson put it, "After that no word was heard from Princeton about the classic Reformed doctrine of the Lord's Supper" (Bard Thompson, "The Catechism and the Mercersburg Theology," in Bard Thompson et al., *Essays on the Heidelberg Catechism* [Philadelphia: United Church, 1963], 70).

Chapter 1. Biblical Foundations of the Lord's Supper
1 Paul Bradshaw, *The Search for the Origins of Christian Worship* (New York: Oxford University Press, 1992), 51, 205.
2 Most scholars today reject the idea that this was a Passover meal. See R. T. France, "Chronological Aspects of 'Gospel Harmony,'" *Vox Evangelica* 16 (1986): 50–54; C. K. Barrett, *The Gospel According to St. John* (London: SPCK, 1978), 48–50; J. Jeremias, *The Eucharistic Words of Jesus* (London:

NOTES

SCM, 1966), 41–62. But see in contrast D. A. Carson, *The Gospel According to John* (Leicester: InterVarsity, 1991), 455–57.

3 See Wayne Grudem, *Systematic Theology* (Grand Rapids: Zondervan, 1994), 988–89.

4 In both cases, the context is ecclesiastical (note the connection with "the apostles' teaching" and "the prayers" in 2:42, and with activities at the temple in the passage and the one following). The churchly setting in 20:7f. is obvious. See F. F. Bruce, *The Acts of the Apostles: The Greek Text with Introduction and Commentary* (London: Tyndale, 1952), 100.

5 Augustine, "Lectures or Tractates on the Gospel According to St. John," 80:3, in J. P. Migne et al., eds., *Patrologia Latina* (Paris, 1878–90), 35:1840; (P. Schaff and H. Wace, eds., *Nicene and Post-Nicene Fathers of the Christian Church* (Edinburgh: T. & T. Clark, 1886–1900), 7:344.

6 Matt. 16:21–28; John 16:1–4; Matt. 24:1–36 (cf. Mark 13:1–31; Luke 21:1–33); Matt. 18:15–20; Matt. 16:13–20.

7 Raymond E. Brown, *The Gospel According to John (i–xii)* (London: Chapman, 1966), 246ff.; C. F. D. Moule, "A Note on *Didache* ix.4," *Journal of Theological Studies* 6 (1955): 240–43.

8 J. Stevenson, ed., and W. H. C. Frend, rev., *A New Eusebius: Documents Illustrating the History of the Church to AD 337* (London: SPCK, 1987), 36, 66, citing Eusebius, *Ecclesiastical History*, and Athenagoras, *Legatio pro Christianis*.

9 George R. Beasley-Murray, *John*, Word Biblical Commentary (Waco, Tex.: Word, 1987), 94–95. Beasley-Murray doubts that the words of institution underlie this discourse, but acknowledges that neither the evangelist nor his readers could have written or read this passage without consciously referring to the Lord's Supper. Carson shows confusion over the sacraments, appearing to see the alternatives here as a physical eating and drinking or a purely spiritual and metaphorical interpretation. In doing so, he distinguishes sharply between metaphorical and nonmetaphorical language, asserting that the meaning of the discourse lies with the former and does not refer to the eucharist at all. He misses the point that both metaphorical and nonmetaphorical elements are present in the sacraments. Even so, he agrees that no passage in Scripture unfolds the meaning of the eucharist as clearly as this (D. A. Carson, *The Gospel According to John* [Leicester: InterVarsity, 1991], 288–98). On the other hand, Raymond E. Brown argues that the eucharist is a secondary theme, in his *The Gospel According to John*

NOTES

(i–xii) (London: Chapman, 1966), 282–83, 291–92. Barnabas Lindars claims that the sacraments are presupposed by John, *The Gospel of John* (London: Marshall, Morgan & Scott, 1972), 59. Rudolph Schnackenberg points out that recent work on John has demonstrated that the words of institution lie behind the discourse, in his *The Gospel According to John*, vol. 2 (London: Burns & Oates, 1980), 55. See also Ernst Haenchen, *The Gospel of John*, vol. 1 (Philadelphia: Fortress, 1984), 294f.

10 Lesslie Newbigin, *The Light Has Come: An Exposition of the Fourth Gospel* (Grand Rapids: Eerdmans, 1982), 84–85.

11 Cf. Raymond E. Brown, *John (i–xii)*, 282–83, 291–92.

12 John Calvin, *Institutes of the Christian Religion*, ed. John T. McNeill, 4.17.9.

Chapter 2. The Lord's Supper in Church History

1 Justin Martyr, "Apology," 1.66, in Alexander Roberts and James Donaldson, eds., *The Ante-Nicene Fathers* (reprint, Edinburgh: T.&T. Clark, 1993), 1:185. But note that this passage is ambiguous and has been claimed by Lutherans and Protestants as well.

2 That it was not universal in the Western church until later is evident in the work of the ninth-century monk Ratramn (d. 868), in his *De Corpore et Sanguine Domini*. He stresses that the elements remain unchanged (xii–xiii), that John 6 is not to be taken corporally (xxix–xxxiii), that the sovereign power of the Holy Spirit is necessary (xxvi–xxxi), and that Christ is eaten spiritually not physically (lix–lxii). As bread and wine nourish and intoxicate human beings, so the Word of God who is the living bread revives the minds of believers (xl). See *Ratramnus, De Corpore et Sanguine Domini: Texte Original et Notice Bibliographique* (Amsterdam, North-Holland: Series Verhandeligen der Koninklijke Nederlandse Akademie van Wetershappen, 1974).

3 Richard A. Muller, *Dictionary of Latin and Greek Theological Terms Drawn Principally from Protestant Scholasticism* (Grand Rapids: Baker, 1985), 18–19, 290–91.

4 See Johannes Quasten, *Patrology*, vol. 2, *The Ante-Nicene Literature after Irenaeus* (reprint, Westminster, Md.: Christian Classics, 1992), 85–87; Cyprian, "On the Sacrament of the Cup of the Lord," in Roberts and Donaldson, eds., *The Ante-Nicene Fathers*, 5:358–64. The Cyprian work is also known as *Epistolus 63*.

5 See John W. Nevin, *The Mystical Presence* (Philadelphia, 1846), passim.

NOTES

6 Cited in Iain H. Murray, *The Forgotten Spurgeon* (London: Banner of Truth, 1966), 139.

7 Despite the qualifications made by the *Catechism of the Catholic Church* (London: Geoffrey Chapman, 1994), 259, where it states that "the fruits of the sacraments also depend on the disposition of the one who receives them."

8 Ibid., 313.

9 B. J. Kidd, ed., *Documents Illustrative of the Continental Reformation* (Oxford: Clarendon, 1911), 247–54.

10 Formula of Concord (1576), Art. 7.1–11, Art. 8.11–12, in Phillip Schaff, ed., *The Creeds of Christendom* (1877; reprint, Grand Rapids: Baker, 1966), 3:137–40.

11 See W. P. Stephens, *The Theology of Huldrych Zwingli* (Oxford: Clarendon, 1986), 194–259. For Zwingli on baptism, see my article "Baptism in the Writings of the Reformers," *Scottish Bulletin of Evangelical Theology* 7 (1989): 21–44.

12 See Robert Letham, *The Work of Christ* (Leicester: Inter-Varsity; Downers Grove, Ill.: InterVarsity, 1993), 211–20; and, "Is Evangelicalism Christian?" *Evangelical Quarterly* 67 (1995): 3–33, with the rejoinder by Donald MacLeod of Free Church College, Edinburgh, and my surrejoinder.

13 See Letham, *The Work of Christ,* 105–24.

14 See John Calvin, *Institutes of the Christian Religion,* ed. John T. McNeill, 2.13.4. For a fuller discussion of this point, see E. David Willis, *Calvin's Catholic Christology: The Function of the So-Called "Extra-Calvinisticum" in Calvin's Theology* (Leiden: E. J. Brill, 1966). Willis presents overwhelming evidence that this was classic patristic teaching and could as well be called the "extra-patristicum."

15 Robert Bruce, *The Mystery of the Lord's Supper,* trans. and ed. Thomas F. Torrance (London: James Clarke, 1958), 44–46.

Chapter 3. The Lord's Supper in Reformed Theology

1 Robert Bruce, *The Mystery of the Lord's Supper,* trans. and ed. Thomas F. Torrance (London: James Clarke, 1958), 79; cf. also 62, 90–92.

2 Phillip Schaff, ed., *The Creeds of Christendom* (1877; reprint, Grand Rapids: Baker, 1966), 3:307–479.

3 Paul E. Rorem, "The *Consensus Tigurinus* (1549): Did Calvin Compromise?" in Wilhelm H. Neuser, ed., *Calvinus Sacrae Scripturae Professor: Calvin as Confessor of Holy Scripture* (Grand Rapids: Eerdmans, 1994), 72–90.

NOTES

4 John Calvin, *Institutes of the Christian Religion*, ed. John T. McNeill, 4.17.3.

5 Ibid., 4.17.5.

6 John Calvin, *Short Treatise on the Holy Supper of Our Lord and Only Saviour Jesus Christ*, in J. K. S. Reid, ed., *Calvin: Theological Treatises* (Philadelphia: Westminster, 1954), 144. Hereafter *ST*.

7 Ibid.

8 Ibid., 145–46.

9 Ibid., 146–48.

10 D. W. Torrance and T. F. Torrance, eds., *Calvin's Commentaries: The Epistles of Paul the Apostle to the Galatians, Ephesians, Philippians and Colossians* (Grand Rapids: Eerdmans, 1965), 208–10.

11 Calvin, *Institutes* 4.17.8–10; *ST* 166.

12 Martin Bucer, *Ennarationum in evangelia Matthaei, Marci et Lucae libri duo* (Strassburg, 1527), 244a.; *Bericht* aa.3. a.6–9.; Pietro Martire Vermigli, *Disputatio de eucharistiae sacramento in celeberrime Angliae schola Oxoniensi habitae* (London, 1549); idem, *Tractatio de sacramento eucharistiae, habita in Universitate Oxoniensi* (London, 1549); idem, *Defensio doctrinae veteris et apostolicae sacrosancto eucharistiae sacramento adversus Stephani Gardineri* (Zürich, 1559); Robert Bruce, *The Mystery of the Lord's Supper*, trans. and ed. Thomas F. Torrance (London: James Clarke, 1958), 52, 82; Amandus Polanus, *Partitiones theologiae* (Basel, 1590), 149, 277–82; idem, *Syntagma theologiae Christianae* (Hanover, 1609), 2925–30, 3220–26; Guilielmus Bucanus, *Institutiones theologiae* (n.p., 1604), 769–88. Robert L. Reymond fails to appreciate that this was not merely Calvin's personal position but that of classic Reformed theology as a whole; see his book *A New Systematic Theology of the Christian Faith* (Nashville: Thomas Nelson, 1998), 961–64. See Joseph C. McLelland, *The Visible Words of God: An Exposition of the Sacramental Theology of Peter Martyr Vermigli AD 1500–1562* (Edinburgh: Oliver and Boyd, 1957), 280, who concludes that Martyr, Bucer, and Calvin were at one on the Lord's Supper.

13 Calvin, *Institutes* 4.17.11–15, cf. 39; *ST* 155–61.

14 Calvin, *Institutes* 4.17.16–27.

15 Ibid., 4.17.31.

16 Ibid., 4.17.32.

17 Ibid., 4.17.33.

18 Calvin, *ST* 149.

NOTES

19   Ibid., 150.

20   Calvin, *Institutes* 4.17.38.

21   Calvin, *ST* 154.

22   Ibid., 152; *Institutes* 4.17.42.

23   *ST* 153; *Institutes* 4.17.44.

24   See the *Oxford English Dictionary*.

25   Schaff, *Creeds of Christendom*, 3:507.

26   See *The Catechism of the Catholic Church* (London: Geoffrey Chapman, 1994), 306–9.

27   On the problems of individualism in the Western world and its effect on the Christian church, see inter alia Robert Letham, *The Work of Christ* (Leicester: Inter-Varsity; Downers Grove, Ill.: InterVarsity, 1993), and "Is Evangelicalism Christian?" *Evangelical Quarterly* 67 (1995); Bruce, *Mystery of the Lord's Supper*, 108.

Chapter 4. The Lord's Supper in Practice

1   Robert Letham, *The Work of Christ* (Leicester: Inter-Varsity; Downers Grove, Ill.: InterVarsity, 1993), 91–102.

2   The Second Helvetic Confession, ch. 1, in Formula of Concord (1576), Art. 7.1–11, Art. 8.11–12, in Phillip Schaff, ed., *The Creeds of Christendom* (1877; reprint, Grand Rapids: Baker, 1966), 3:237–88, 831–33.

3   Letham, *The Work of Christ*, 99.

4   See Karl Barth, *Church Dogmatics* (Edinburgh: T.&T. Clark, 1956, 1975), I/1–2.

5   See further, Robert Bruce, *The Mystery of the Lord's Supper*, trans. and ed. Thomas F. Torrance (London: James Clarke, 1958), 107–8, 112–13.

6   Both here and in the case below of multiple cups I do not mean to imply that the sacrament is nullified by these practices as if its essence depended on precision in the smallest detail. However, there is little doubt that these are irregularities. The keynote must always be faithfulness to Christ in matters large and small.

7   Bruce, *Mystery of the Lord's Supper*, 109–10.

8   "*Methyskō* demonstrates some inebriation was involved" but "John's point is simply that the wine Jesus provides is unqualifiedly superior, as must everything be that is tied to the new messianic age Jesus is introducing" (D. A. Carson, *The Gospel According to John*, [Leicester: InterVarsity, 1991], 174–75).

NOTES

9 Paul Bradshaw, *The Search for the Origins of Christian Worship* (New York: Oxford University Press, 1992), 205.

10 Wayne Grudem, *Systematic Theology* (Grand Rapids: Zondervan, 1994), 988–89.

11 Bradshaw, *The Search for the Origins of Christian Worship*, 51.

12 A. A. Hodge, *Outlines of Theology* (reprint, Grand Rapids: Zondervan, 1972), 633.

13 John Calvin, *Institutes of the Christian Religion*, ed. John T. McNeill, 4.17.43.

14 A. A. Hodge, *Outlines of Theology*, 634.

15 See Timothy Ware, *The Orthodox Church* (London: Penguin, 1963), 295.

16 "The Lord's Supper is to be administered often . . . and that only to such as are of years and ability to examine themselves."

17 See further Bruce, *Mystery of the Lord's Supper*, 47, 49, 67.

18 J. H. S. Burleigh, *A Church History of Scotland* (London: Oxford University Press, 1960), 163.

19 Richard L. Greaves, *Theology and Revolution in the Scottish Reformation* (Grand Rapids: Christian University Press, 1980), 107. Greaves points out that Knox's preference for frequent communion is akin to Luther's and Calvin's and the English Reformers'. See also Norman Sykes, *The Crisis of the Reformation* (London: Centenary, 1946), 55, 68, 91–92.

20 John Calvin, *Short Treatise on the Holy Supper of Our Lord and Only Saviour Jesus Christ*, in J. K. S. Reid, ed., *Calvin: Theological Treatises* (Philadelphia: Westminster, 1954), 153.

21 John Calvin, *Articles Concerning the Organization of the Church and Worship at Geneva Proposed by Ministers at the Council January 16, 1537* in J. K. S. Reid, ed., *Calvin: Theological Treatises*, 49. See also *Institutes* 4.17.43: "The Supper could have been administered most becomingly if it were set before the church very often, and at least once a week."

22 Wulfert de Greef, *The Writings of John Calvin: An Introductory Guide*, trans. Lyle D. Bierma (Grand Rapids: Baker, 1993), 144–45. See also Ronald S. Wallace, *Calvin's Doctrine of the Word and Sacrament* (Edinburgh: Oliver & Boyd, 1953), 253.

23 Diarmaid MacCulloch, *Thomas Cranmer: A Life* (New Haven: Yale University Press, 1996).

24 James C. Spalding, *The Reformation of the Ecclesiastical Laws of England, 1552*, Sixteenth Century Essays & Studies, 19 (Kirksville, Mo.: Sixteenth Century Journal Publishers, 1992), 120, 122.

NOTES

25 "The Directory for the Public Worship of God," in *The Confession of Faith* (Applecross, Rossshire: The Publications Committee of the Free Presbyterian Church of Scotland, 1970), 384.

26 Bruce, *Mystery of the Lord's Supper*, 56.

Epilogue: The Lord's Supper and the Future

1 "The Order for Holy Communion: Also Called the Eucharist and the Lord's Supper: Rite A," in *A Shorter Alternative Service Book: Services from the Alternative Service Book, 1980. Authorized for Use in the Church of England in Conjunction with the Book of Common Prayer* (Cambridge: Cambridge University Press, 1980), 139.

2 Aidan Nichols, O.P., "St. Thomas Aquinas on the Passion of Christ: A Reading of *Summa Theologiae* IIIa, q.46," *Scottish Journal of Theology* 43 (1990): 447–59.

INDEX
OF SCRIPTURE

INDEX OF SCRIPTURE